SIMPLY Classics

INTERMEDIATE

Bridal Chorus

Richard Wagner

AF732262

Arranged for Piano Solo by Allan Small

Alfred

One of the greatest composers and librettists that ever lived, Richard Wagner (1813–1883) is perhaps best known for his operatic works. This familiar piece comes from the wedding scene in Wagner's musical drama *Lohengrin*.

Bridal Chorus

from *Lohengrin*

Richard Wagner
(1813–1883)
Arr. Allan Small

Copyright © MCMXCV by Alfred Publishing Co., Inc.
All rights reserved. Printed in USA.

(a) Go back to the beginning and play until Fine.

SIMPLY

Classics

These popular themes and well-known classics have been skillfully adapted for the growing pianist, but still retain the essential beauty and style of the original works. These solos are the perfect repertoire for elementary- to intermediate-level students, allowing them to enjoy the timeless classics of the masters at an earlier stage in their musical development.

C.P.E. Bach
Solfeggietto (12887)

J. S. Bach
Jesu, Joy of Man's Desiring (12888)

Bach/Gounod
Avé Maria (14306)

Beethoven
Für Elise (12889)
Ode to Joy (Theme from Symphony No. 9) (14352)
Theme from the Moonlight Sonata (12890)
Theme from the Second Movement of Sonata Pathétique (14301)

Berlin
Alexander's Ragtime Band (14311)

Bizet
Gypsy Dance (14312)
Toreador Song (14326)

Brahms
Hungarian Dance No. 5 (16701)
Lullaby (14302)
Waltz Op. 39, No. 15 (14323)

Chopin
"Minute Waltz" (Waltz, Op. 64, No. 1) (14337)
Nocturne in E-Flat Op. 9, No.2 (14328)
Prelude Op. 28, No. 4 (14313)
Theme from Polonaise, Op. 53 (14354)
Theme from the Fantasy-Impromptu (14304)
Theme from the First Ballade (14327)
Theme from the Op. 10, No. 3 Etude (14303)
Theme from the Third Movement of Sonata, Op. 35 (14338)
Valse Theme, Op. 70, No. 1 (14349)
Waltz in D Minor (16709)

Cohan
Give My Regards to Broadway (14325)
The Yankee Doodle Boy (14353)

Debussy
Clair de lune (12891)
First Arabesque (14347)
La fille aux cheveux de lin (The Girl with the Flaxen Hair) (14355)
Le petit Nègre (Cakewalk) (14351)
Reverie (12892)

Elgar
Pomp and Circumstance No. 1 (16703)

Ellmenreich
Spinning Song (14305)

Grieg
In the Hall of the Mountain King (14329)
Theme from the Piano Concerto (12893)

Joplin
The Easy Winners (14307)
Elite Syncopations (14345)
The Entertainer (12894)
Maple Leaf Rag (14330)
Solace (16702)

Lincke
The Glowworm (16708)

Liszt
Liebestraum No. 3 (16700)
Theme from Hungarian Rhapsody No. 2 (14339)
Un Sospiro (14321)

Marchetti
Fascination (16705)

Martini
Plaisir d'amour (14340)

Mendelssohn
Wedding March (14314)

Mozart
Opening Theme from Symphony No. 40 (14341)
Rondo alla Turca (14315)
Theme from Piano Concerto No. 21 (14308)
Theme from Sonata in C Major, K. 545 (14350)
Variations on "Ah! vous dirai-je, maman" (Twinkle, Twinkle, Little Star) (14356)

Mussorgsky
Great Gate of Kiev (14346)

Pachelbel
Theme from the Celebrated Canon in D (12895)

Paderewski
Minuet in G (14316)

Puccini
Musetta's Waltz (14317)

Rachmaninoff
Theme from the Second Piano Concerto (12896)
Theme from the Op. 3, No. 2 Prelude (14310)
Rhapsody on a Theme of Paganini (14322)

Rossini
William Tell Overture (14342)

Saint-Saëns
The Swan (14318)

Schubert
Impromptu Op. 142, No. 2 (14324)
Theme from Marche Militaire (14343)
Theme from Unfinished Symphony (14319)

Schumann
Chopin (from Carnaval) (14357)

Sousa
The Stars and Stripes Forever! (16707)

Tchaikovsky
June: Barcarolle (from The Seasons) (14348)
Theme from the Fifth Symphony (16706)
Theme from the First Piano Concerto (14320)

Verdi
La Donna è Mobile from Rigoletto (16704)

Wagner
Bridal Chorus from Lohengrin (14309)

ISBN-10: 0-7390-2850-2
ISBN-13: 978-0-7390-2852-6
9 780739 028506

Alfred
alfred.com

9780739028506
TP
APEX

A Kalmus Classic Edition

Béla

BARTÓK

SKETCHES

Opus 9

FOR PIANO

K 03138

Kalmus